Published in Great Britain in MMXVII by
Book House, an imprint of
The Salariya Book Company Ltd
25 Marlborough Place, Brighton BN1 1UB
www.salariya.com

ISBN: 978-1-910706-66-4

SALARIYA

1 3 5 7 9 8 6 4 2

A CIP catalogue record for this book is available
from the British Library.

Printed and bound in China.

BEE

Louise & Richard
Spilsbury

UP CLOSE &
SCARY

BOOK HOUSE
a SALARIYA imprint

Contents

Bees

Bees are furry, flying **insects** that can give people and other animals a nasty sting. There are around 25,000 different **species**, or types, of bee in the world. Some species live alone but honeybees and bumblebees live in groups called **colonies**. They build nests called **hives**.

The queen bee lays her eggs in a hive. She remains here with her **larvae**. The **worker bees** build the hive, collect food and care for the larvae and the queen bee. They leave the hive to collect **pollen** and a sweet juice, called **nectar**, from flowers. They eat the pollen and turn it into a food for the larvae to eat. They take the nectar back to the hive to eat and to make honey.

A hive can contain 60,000 to 80,000 bees.

Worker bees are the only bees usually seen flying around outside the nest.

Most bees have black and yellow stripes. These colours send a warning to other animals that bees can give them a painful sting.

The body

Like other insects, the bee's body is made up of three main parts: the head, **thorax** and **abdomen**. The body is covered in a hard outer coat, called an **exoskeleton**, which protects its insides. The bee's **muscles** are attached to the inside of the exoskeleton. The thick fuzzy hair on its body helps to keep it warm in cold weather. Pollen sticks to the bee's hair when it lands in a flower.

Superpowers

When a honeybee finds food, it tells other workers in the hive where to find it by doing a 'bee dance'. By flying in a circle or a figure-of-eight pattern and waggling its body, it can indicate the direction, distance, size and quality of the food source. The food can be up to 5 km (3 miles) away. Imagine being able to communicate all that with a waggle of your hips!

8

As the bee dances, it waggles its abdomen to indicate how far away the flowers are.

When a food source is very close to the hive, the bee's dance is performed by moving in circles.

The angle of the bee's dance in relation to the sun, tells other bees the direction of the food.

Bees can also use their waggle dance to tell other bees if there are any dangerous **predators** near the food source.

9

The abdomen

The bee's abdomen contains two stomachs. One stomach is used to **digest** nectar. The second stomach is a honey sac that is used to carry nectar back to the hive. A bee's stinger is at the end of its abdomen. This sharp stinger pierces the skin and delivers **venom** into the victim's body. A bee will sting only to protect its colony or when it is frightened.

Honeybees sting only once. They die afterwards because the stinger remains stuck inside the victim's skin and pulls out part of the bee's abdomen as the bee flies away.

The honeybee stinger is hollow and pointed, like a needle.

The stinger has two rows of saw-toothed hooks or blades to cut through the victim's skin.

The stinger hooks are angled. Once they are in a victim's body, they are hard to pull out.

Superpowers

The abdomen holds the secret to another bee superpower. Bees can find their way in the dark because substances inside their abdomen can sense the Earth's **magnetic field**. If humans had this superpower, it would be like having a built-in compass that they could use to **navigate** by. People would never need a map again.

The antennae

The **antennae** are found on the bee's head between its eyes. The antennae can do many amazing things. They are packed with **sense organs** that can smell, taste and feel. They can smell flowers and taste food. They sense the **vibrations** in the air made by bees when they dance. They also pick up the scents or smells that bees use to communicate. Antennae can sense wind direction and speed, so bees can work out how to fly faster, and how and where to land.

Superpowers

Some scientists think bees use their right antenna to tell the difference between bees from their own colony and those from another hive. Humans would have to be mind readers to be able to tell everything about someone without even speaking to them.

The many tiny hairs on the antennae are sensors, which detect scent and vibrations.

Bees have two antennae to work out which direction a smell comes from and how far away it is. If a smell is stronger to one antenna than the other, it means the smell is closer to that side.

Bumblebees and honeybees have a **joint** in their antennae. This joint enables the antennae to bend in different directions.

The antennae usually have 12 or 13 segments.

The eyes

If you look at a close-up of a bee's face, you can see five eyes staring back at you. A bee has three **simple eyes** and two **compound eyes**. The three simple eyes look like shiny bumps and they act as light sensors. They help the bee to see the sun, even when clouds are hiding it. The bee uses its eyes to spot brightly coloured flower petals.

The compound eyes are made up of hundreds of little hexagonal units called **ommatidia**.

Superpowers

Bees can see things that are invisible to humans, including *ultraviolet* (UV) *light*. Many petals have ultraviolet lined patterns on them that guide the bees towards the flower's nectar stores. Bees can see these patterns clearly but humans cannot see them at all.

14

Each ommatidia has its own **lens**. The images it collects combine with the other lenses to form one whole picture.

The ommatidia are packed closely together but each one looks in a slightly different direction.

A bee's eyes cover most of the surface of its head.

The mouth

Up close, a bee's mouthparts might look scary, but they are very useful. Inside the bee's mouth, fat mixes with saliva (spit) and other ingredients, such as soil or pollen, to make wax. It uses the wax to build the hexagonal cells that fit together to make a hive. A bee uses its stretchy tongue to drink and lick up nectar, honey or water, and to pass on liquid to other bees.

Mandible

The **mandibles** are the bee's strong jaws. It uses them to cut and shape wax, to feed the larvae and the queen, to clean the hive, to fight, to **groom** and to eat pollen.

Labial palp

Maxilla

The bee's long tongue has a hairy tip to help it to lap up food and water. It curls up when not in use.

Tongue

The tongue folds up into the labial palp and maxilla when not in use.

Superpowers

A bumblebee's tongue is amazing. It can reach up to 2 cm (0.8 inches) long when fully stretched, which is as long as its body. If a 6 foot-tall man had a tongue like this, it would be more than 92 cm (one yard) long. With a tongue as long as his arm, imagine how quickly he could lap up a drink!

17

The wings

Bees use their wings to fly and can travel at a speed of around 25 kph (16 mph). Their wings can beat 200 to 230 times per second. Bees also use their wings to keep the hive at a steady temperature. If the hive is too hot, the bees at the entrance flap their wings to waft in cool air.

Bee wings are transparent but they can look silvery when light strikes them at an angle.

Superpowers

Bees have incredible flying power. Each bee usually flies about 1.6 km (1 mile) from the hive each day, but they can fly up to 8 km (5 miles) to collect food. That means a big colony flies a distance equivalent to travelling as far as the moon every day!

18

Bee wings beat very fast so they can fly quickly and hover in one spot.

The front and back wings have hooks. The wings hook together so that they can beat as one when the bee is flying. The wings unhook and fold away when the bee is not flying.

The buzzing sound made by bees is actually the sound of their wings beating quickly.

19

The legs

When they land on flowers, bees walk towards nectar stores and pollen. They also use their legs to help them to shape soft wax into the cells of their **honeycomb**. Bees have a groove on their legs that can be rubbed over their antennae to clean off pollen and dust, ensuring that the sensitive antennae keep working properly.

These hairs can form a basket for collecting pollen.

This is a press that helps the bee to pack pollen into the pollen baskets.

In the summer, a worker bee can carry two big pouches full of golden pollen on its legs.

20

This small groove is used to remove pollen from the bee's antennae.

The claws help a bee to grip surfaces and hold things.

Superpowers

A bee's back legs carry pollen to the hive. They use them to brush pollen onto hairless patches. These patches on the legs are surrounded by stiff hairs that form a basket. When a bee's legs are loaded with pollen and it has a stomach full of nectar, its cargo equals its own body weight. An aeroplane can take off only with a cargo of up to a quarter of its weight!

Queen bee

Most hives have only one queen. The queen **mates** with male bees called drones, who live only for a short time and have no other job to do for their colony. The queen bee lays eggs and releases scents called **pheromones**. Only the bees in the queen's hive can smell these. The pheromones tell the bees that their queen is still alive and that all is well in the hive.

A queen bee is much bigger than a worker bee. However, her brain is smaller because her only job is to lay eggs.

Superpowers

A queen can lay about one egg every 20 seconds. In summer, a queen lays about 2,000 eggs, day and night. That means she lays her own body weight in eggs every 24 hours. If humans had that many babies, there would not be enough room on the planet for everyone to live.

22

If a queen bee dies, the workers create a new queen by choosing a young larva and feeding it a special food, called royal jelly, to make it grow into a queen bee.

Queen bee

Pheromones are such an efficient way of communicating that if a queen leaves the hive, all the bees in the colony know about it within 15 minutes.

Leafcutter bees

Leafcutter bees live alone. They are so named because they cut leaves to build their nests in the holes found in rotting wood or plant stems. A leafcutter bee uses its mandibles to bite off pieces of leaf. It uses these pieces to create cell walls inside a barrel-shaped nest. It collects pollen and nectar to put inside each cell along with the larvae, so that they have enough food to grow into adults.

Leafcutter bees are black and about the size of a honeybee.

The underside of the abdomen often looks yellow because pollen is carried on stiff hairs there, rather than on their legs.

Superpowers

After cutting a piece of leaf, leafcutter bees fly back to the nest, clutching the leaf to the underside of their body. They are strong enough to carry a piece of leaf as big, if not bigger, than themselves. Just imagine if you walked around all day carrying objects bigger than yourself.

Leafcutter bees cut very neat circles or ovals from the edge of leaves. These measure about 1.9 cm (0.75 inch) in diameter.

Killer bees

Africanised honeybees are known as killer bees because they are so scary! They behave normally when they are hunting for food but if they sense that their colony is in danger, they will defend it ferociously. When a large swarm of killer bees attacks people or animals it can kill because the swarm delivers up to 2,000 stings at once.

Killer bees are dangerous. While only about one in ten honeybees might attack to defend their hive, the whole colony of Africanised honeybees will attack if its hive is disturbed. By disturbing a honeybee colony you might get a few stings, but if you disturb an Africanised colony, you will get hundreds of stings!

Superpowers

Killer bees are deadly. When they sting, a chemical alarm is also given off. This alerts the other bees in their colony to danger and makes them swarm and attack. Killer bees react to disturbances ten times faster than European honeybees, and they will chase people 0.4 km (0.25 miles) before they stop!

Once disturbed, colonies may stay on alert for up to 24 hours, attacking people and animals that they find near the hive.

The pheromones released by killer bees to tell the rest of the colony to attack, smell like bananas.

It does not take much for killer bees to be disturbed and for their alarm systems to be activated.

Killer bees were developed in a laboratory in Brazil. Scientists were trying to breed European honeybees with African bees to create a bee that would produce more honey. Instead, they created a less productive and highly aggressive species.

That's scary!

The truly scary thing about bees is that they are dying out. In the United States, more than half of all honeybee nests have disappeared. Some bees are dying because of **climate change**. As parts of the world become hotter, the heat is killing bees. Bees are also dying because trees are cut down and countryside is cleared, leaving fewer places for nests and fewer flowers to visit.

Bees make honey and **pollinate** plants. They mix nectar and saliva in their mouths to make a liquid that turns into honey in the hive cells. They make two to three times more honey than they need, so people can take some to eat. When bees move between flowers, they transfer pollen between the male and female parts of different flowers, allowing plants to grow seeds and fruit.

Superpowers

We need a lot of bees to make the honey we eat. Most worker bees live for about six weeks and make around one-twelfth of a teaspoon of honey. The bees in one colony have to fly about 88,514 km (55,000 miles) to make just 0,4 kg (1 pound) of honey – that is nearly seven times around the world!

28

Bees are vital – we need them. They pollinate three-quarters of the world's most important crops.

Glossary

Abdomen stomach.

Antennae a pair of sense organs located near the front of an insect's head.

Climate change the gradual increase in the Earth's temperature, thought to be caused by human actions, such as burning oil, gas and coal.

Colonies groups.

Compound eyes eyes made up of many lenses.

Digest to break down food to be absorbed into the body.

Exoskeleton the hard outer covering on the outside of an animal's body.

Groom to clean or brush dust from an animal's body.

Hives nests built by bees.

Honeycomb a structure of hexagonal cells of wax that forms the inside of a hive.

Insects animals with six legs and a body divided into three sections: head, thorax and abdomen. Some insects also have wings.

Joint a place where two bones or body parts that can move separately, meet.

Larvae the wingless, often wormlike, form of insects when first hatched from eggs.

Lens the part of an eye that gathers light so an animal can see.

Magnetic field the area around a magnetic object where magnetic forces can be felt. The Earth has a magnetic field because it contains magnetic metals in its core.

Mandibles jaws.

Mates comes together to breed and create young.

Muscles the parts of the body that can make an animal move.

Navigate to find one's way.

Nectar a sugary juice found in the centre of a flower's petals.

Ommatidia the units that make up a compound eye.

Pheromones chemicals that are released to send signals to other animals.

Pollen a fine powder that flowers make.

Pollinate when pollen from one flower moves to another flower of the same kind, to make seeds and develop fruit.

Predators animals that hunt other animals to eat.

Sense organs body parts that give an animal one or more of the five senses (sight, hearing, smell, taste and touch).

Simple eyes eyes with only one lens.

Species a type of animal or plant.

Thorax the chest or part of an animal's body between its head and its abdomen.

Ultraviolet (UV) light a form of light energy that humans cannot see.

Venom poison that animals make to kill prey or defend themselves.

Vibrations movements up and down and to and fro.

Worker bees the female bees that do all the work in a colony.

Index